Hackers

David Orme

Text © David Orme 2001

The right of David Orme to be identified as author of this work has been asserted by him in accordance with the Copyright, Designs and Patents Act 1988.

All rights reserved. No part of this publication may be reproduced or transmitted in any form or by any means, electronic or mechanical, including photocopy, recording or any information storage and retrieval system, without permission in writing from the publisher or under licence from the Copyright Licensing Agency Limited. Further details of such licences (for reprographic reproduction) may be obtained from the Copyright Licensing Agency Limited, 90 Tottenham Court Road, London W1T 4LP.

First published in 2001 by:
Nelson Thornes Ltd
Delta Place
27 Bath Road
CHELTENHAM
GL53 7TH
United Kingdom

01 02 03 04 05 / 10 9 8 7 6 5 4 3 2 1

A catalogue record for this book is available from the British Library.

ISBN 0-7487-6071-7

Cover artwork by Martin Berry
Typeset by Tech-Set Ltd, Gateshead
Printed and bound in Great Britain by Martins The Printers Ltd, Berwick upon Tweed

1

Date: Friday, 15 April 1994
Location: Air Force Information Warfare Centre, Texas, USA

The lights were dim in the deep, underground room. Faces glowed in the light of computer screens. Two hundred metres above, fighter planes got ready for action. Rockets waited for the codes to send them to war. A war that would be the last in the history of the world . . .

General Hobbs sat at his desk. Below him were rows of computers. He hated them. In the old days you knew who your enemies were and where they were coming from. But now they attacked you through your own computers.

They were like rats sneaking in through the drains of a house. They wiped out files and spread the country's secrets around on the Internet for anyone to read. At one time, no one would dare to attack a great country like the United States. Now it seemed that any enemy with a cheap computer and a phone line could take over.

Six agents watched the screens. They'd not left their posts for two weeks. Around the room were drink cans, sleeping bags and leftover food.

Suddenly, a red light flashed and an alarm sounded. The agents crowded around a screen.

'Is that him?' asked the general.

'That's him.'

'How's he getting in?'

'He's got Pentagon codes.'

'But those codes were only changed three days ago...'

'This guy knows what he's doing. He knows when we change them. He knows what we change them to...'

General Hobbs hurried down the steps from his desk. In the USA, you couldn't go higher than the Pentagon. The people in the Pentagon told America when to go to war.

'Report!' he snapped.

'It's him. Datastream Cowboy.'

'What's he doing?'

'Downloading battlefield codes from the Pentagon computers.'

'Can't you kick him out?'

'That wouldn't be a problem. But he'd find a new way to get in. We'd have to start all over again. The only way to track him down is to let him run with it. Once he makes a mistake, we've got him!'

'Have you found anything new?'

The agent shook his head. 'No. He's clever, this one. He seems to move around – South Africa, Italy, South America. He never uses one phone line long enough to let us get a handle on him. He could be anywhere in the world.'

'So, we're counting on him to make a mistake. What if he doesn't make one?'

'He will. They always do.'

Another alarm sounded.

'He's moved. He's left the Pentagon system.'

'Where is he now?'

The agents watched as a string of words and figures moved up the screen. The screen settled down. A single line of code flashed.

'Oh my God! It's the Hanscom Air Force Base. He's cracked it right open.'

The screen changed again. Letters and numbers flicked up in a mad dance.

'What's going on?' shouted the general. 'What's he after?'

'He's after the rocket codes.'

2

Date: March and April 1994
Location: The Pentagon, Washington DC, USA

Datastream Cowboy's name had first been seen on the Pentagon's computer screens two weeks before. A sharp-eyed manager had noticed something strange. A code was being used from two different places. When the hacker started downloading files, army chiefs knew they had a big problem on their hands.

The Pentagon staff work in what is probably the most guarded building in the world. They are used to hackers trying to get into their system. They said attacks were running at 250,000 a year. Most of these were stopped early on. But not Datastream Cowboy's.

At first, it wasn't clear if there was just one hacker or more. The attacks came through phone lines from all over the world. These were bounced to the USA by satellite. Experts were soon able to spot the hacker from the way he worked. After a week or so, he even signed his name – 'Datastream Cowboy'.

Now he'd got into the Pentagon, he could find the codes to link him to every US base in the world. He could send his messages through the Pentagon system. When a message came from the Pentagon, everyone believed it. If the message said 'fire the rockets', the rockets flew. And the world was at war.

Army chiefs had a top-level meeting. One thing was clear – Datastream Cowboy knew just the information he wanted. That was the information the USA didn't want its enemies to have. But who was behind Datastream Cowboy? The Russians? The Chinese? Whoever it was, this was the greatest danger the USA had ever faced.

Things got even worse when the hacker reached a power plant in Korea. For a while there was a panic. Cowboy was hacking into a Korean nuclear plant, using a Pentagon computer. North Korea was an enemy country.
An attack on its computer system would be seen as war. And North Korea had nuclear weapons . . .

Everyone felt better when they found out that the nuclear power plant was in friendly South Korea. But it had been a close thing. Next time perhaps they wouldn't be so lucky. This hacker had to be found – fast!

A team of six computer experts was set up. They watched the system night and day. Again and again they saw the tell-tale signs of a visit from Datastream Cowboy. But whatever they did, they couldn't find out where his attacks were coming from. He was an expert at covering his tracks.

Then one day they found out something that might just lead to the hacker. He had a friend!

One of the experts explained it to General Hobbs.

'Two or three times Datastream Cowboy hasn't been able to get into one of the sites. Then he's sent an e-mail to someone he calls Kuji. This Kuji must be a top man. He tells Cowboy what to do. When Cowboy comes back, he knows exactly how to get in!'

Could this be the clue they needed? Who was Kuji? Could either of the hackers be found before every part of the American computer network had been broken into?

The US Government was asked for vast sums of money for new computer systems. They agreed to pay up. They didn't have a choice. An American leader described what could happen if the US computer system crashed.

'Everyday life now depends on computer systems. Banking, trade, air traffic control, even hospitals – they all need computers. It's not just the army. An attack on our networks could cause more damage to this country than a nuclear war. And if this country goes down, the rest of the world goes down with us.'

3

Date: Friday, 15 April 1994
Location: Air Force Information Warfare Centre, Texas, USA

General Hobbs banged the desk with his fist. He was getting more and more angry about the lack of facts. An empty Coke can jumped up and fell to the floor. The other six men didn't even look up. Their eyes were fixed on the screen.

At last the general could stand it no longer. 'Will someone tell me what the hell's going on? What about those launch codes?'

The agent at the screen looked up and pulled a face.

'Nothing's going on. He's playing games with us. He's done it before.'

'And are we any nearer to getting a fix on him?'

'I'm afraid not.'

'What's he doing now?'

The agent checked the screen. 'He's out of here.' He sat back. 'That's it – we won't be seeing him again for a while.'

The six watchers stood up and stretched themselves. One of them opened a packet of crisps and started to munch them. Another threw himself down on a sleeping bag. A third agent reached for his magazine.

The general shook his head. These men didn't seem to realise how important this was. It might be a game for Datastream Cowboy. He felt it had become a game for the agents too. They needed waking up!

He set off towards the stairs. 'Meeting. Everyone to my office. Now.'

When they'd sat down he looked hard at the team leader. 'So, why can't we track Cowboy down?'

'The only way is to pick up his address from e-mails,' said the team leader. 'The first bit of information on an e-mail is the address of the computer it first came from. We use a trick called fingering to track back to the sender. The trouble is, he knows the trick. You wouldn't believe how well he hides his tracks.'

'OK. Let's have some ideas.'

For a few minutes everyone around the table was silent. Then a quiet man with a beard spoke up. His name was Agent Higgins. 'There's one chance, but it's a long shot.'

'Say it,' growled General Hobbs.

'There's a place where a lot of these hackers hang out. It's called Cyberspace. If either Kuji or Cowboy visit, we might get something.'

'So where is this place?'

'It's a chat room based in Seattle,' explained Higgins. 'Of course, the hackers don't really visit . . .'

The general glared. 'I'm not stupid! I know that! OK, Cyberspace . . . What do the rest of you think?'

The other agents looked at each other and nodded.

'Let's go for it!'

It was agreed. They'd watch the chat room 24 hours a day. Would Datastream Cowboy pay a visit?

A few days later, the leading agent rushed up the stairs to the general's office. 'We've got him! He just talked and talked. He even gave his telephone number!'

The general jumped up from his seat in delight. 'Great! Where is he? Moscow? Cuba?'

The agent shook his head. 'No. He's in London, England.'

4

Date: Wednesday, 11 May 1994
Location: New Scotland Yard, London, UK

Agent Brent Field flew into London from the United States. He was in a secret meeting with a high-ranking British policeman. They were talking about what they had found out so far.

'The calls are coming from a house in North London,' said Chief Inspector Dave Lang of the Metropolitan Police. 'We've had it staked out for three days now. There's nothing special about the house. Nothing to make it stand out from any other.'

Agent Field nodded. 'Sounds like a safe house for a spy to me. Who lives there?'

'The house is owned by a man called Pryce. It says in the records that he mends musical instruments. He lives with his wife, two daughters and 16-year-old son.'

'Could be a cover. What have you learnt from the telephone people?'

'We've put a trace on all calls from the house. He's using a freephone system in Colombia. From there he gets to an Internet service in New York. After that he can go anywhere he wants.'

'We know. Just about every top secret site in the USA. Have there been calls to anywhere else – Russia or China, maybe?'

'No, but we're keeping a watch on it. Of course, he may be using e-mail. That's not so easy to check. We have a system to find out where e-mails are coming from. It's hard getting the go-ahead to use it.'

Agent Field sighed. 'It used to be so much easier. You could tap a phone line, open letters, watch for a place where messages were left. Then the Internet came along.'

Chief Inspector Lang nodded. 'Our own security people have been having problems, too.'

Agent Field sighed again. 'It seems there's no such thing as a secret any more. Of course, we catch a few spies. We put them in jail if we can. The trouble is, anyone can use a computer anywhere in the world. Computer hacking isn't a crime in every country. Sometimes we can't touch the hackers.'

'Well, that isn't the case here. When do you want us to move in?'

'We've got to catch him on line to somewhere he shouldn't be on line to. That's usually in the evening, your time. Be ready to go as soon as we get the call from the States.

13

We're not expecting any trouble, but you'd better have plenty of men ready. Just in case.'

That night, the men staking out the Pryce house waited for the call from the USA. It never came.

Datastream Cowboy was doing nothing inside the house that Chief Inspector Lang could arrest him for.

5

Date: Thursday, 12 May 1994
Time: 20.00 hours
Location: North London, UK

Mrs Pryce had had a funny feeling for some days now. 'There they are again!' she said, looking out of the window.

'Who's there again?' asked Mr Pryce.

'Those men. Sitting in that car over the road.'

'There's no law against sitting in a car.'

'I know that! But they might be thieves planning a break-in. They could be checking on the times people go in and out of their houses.'

'All right. I'll ring the police if you're worried about it.'

'That's another thing. There's something very strange about the phone during the day. There are clicks on the line when you pick it up. And when you're talking.'

'You're lucky you can make a call. I never get a chance to ring anyone in the evening. Richard is always using the line with that computer of his.'

'He says it's very useful for his school work. The phone bill hasn't gone up very much anyway.'

'No, it's strange, that.'

'Richard says he can use freephone numbers or something.'

Just then, Richard put his head around the door. He was Mr and Mrs Pryce's 16-year-old son.

'I'm just going upstairs to log on. Does anyone want to make a phone call before I start?'

'No, that's fine,' said Mr Pryce. 'But don't be all night. Your mother wants me to ring the police. She thinks we've got burglars outside planning a break-in!'

Mr and Mrs Pryce settled down to read in peace.

A car was parked down the road. In it sat Chief Inspector Lang and Sergeant Morris. They were waiting for a call. Around the corner more policemen were waiting for the signal. Would it be tonight?

Suddenly, the call came. The Chief Inspector answered it.

'This is Agent Johnson from the Pentagon. It's him! He's causing big problems over here right now.'

Lang ended the call then keyed in another number. This linked him to a British Telecom officer who was tapping the Pryces' phone.

'Anything from this end?'

'Yes! There's a call from the target number being made to Colombia, South America.'

Lang turned to Sergeant Morris.

'Let's go!'

Quickly, Morris spoke into the car radio. Men from the other cars jumped out. They waited away from the house windows. All the men were armed.

The sergeant was dressed as a parcel delivery man. He crossed the road to the house and knocked on the door.

Inside, the Pryces looked up.

'Who can it be at this time?' Mrs Pryce asked.

Mr Pryce went to the door and opened it. Eight men came out of nowhere and pushed past him into the house.

'What's going on? Who are you? How dare you come in here! I'll call the police!'

'We are the police!' was the answer.

Quickly, the ground floor was searched. Chief Inspector Lang went upstairs. A light was on in one of the bedrooms. He opened the door.

He saw a young man. He was staring hard at the computer screen in front of him. Richard Pryce didn't notice the policeman until his hands were lifted from the keyboard. His eyes opened wide in surprise as his bedroom filled with grim-looking policemen.

'You're under arrest!' said the Chief Inspector.

The shocked teenager sank to the floor and burst into tears.

6

Date: Thursday, 12 May 1994
Time: 21.00 hours
Location: New Scotland Yard, London, UK

'He's only sixteen?' Agent Field could hardly believe his ears.

'That's right. He's just a schoolboy.'

'He must be a computer genius. This kid had the Pentagon in a panic for weeks!'

'Well, I'm not sure what that says about the Pentagon,' said Chief Inspector Lang. 'He's studying music and he only got a grade D in his computer studies exam!'

'You don't say? So what computer was he using?'

'It's down in the labs now. They reckon it's a cheap, out-of-date model. It has very little memory. It probably cost a few hundred pounds from the local computer store.'

Agent Field felt his head was in a spin. 'Are we sure we've got the right person here?'

'He was the one making the phone calls tonight. Anyway, he's downstairs. You'd better come and speak to him yourself.'

Richard Pryce sat behind a desk at New Scotland Yard. His father was with him. Agent Field looked across at the person who had caused all the trouble. He saw a 16-year-old with a tear-stained face. Not the major spy he'd be sent to London to catch.

The Chief Inspector looked across at him. 'Richard, I want you to tell this man everything you've told me.'

Richard took a deep breath. 'It was just a game,' he said. 'I found all these websites about computer hacking. They told you how to get into different computers. There was a lot of hacking software to download. I started with easy targets like colleges. Then I tried harder and harder ones. It was a test to see how far I could go.'

'What about the free phone calls?'

'I found out where to get the software that makes the sounds of dialling codes for phones. I'd phone South America and the software would make the right noises. The operator thought I'd hung up. So, I could make calls to anywhere in the world for free.'

'How did you get into the Pentagon computer?'

'That was easy! The hardest passwords are numbers and letters all mixed up. No one can crack those. But lots of army and air force people don't like them because they can't remember them. They use a one-word password instead. I found this software that could make up 50,000 different passwords a second. I just left the computer running all night. By the morning I'd cracked it. I was in!'

'What was the password?'

'Carmen. I remembered it because it's a famous opera.'

'And why the Pentagon?'

Richard blushed. 'I know it sounds stupid, but I thought I might find out something about UFOs and creatures from outer space. I found out there was information about UFOs at Wright Patterson Air Base. I hacked into there. And into NASA too. I got my messages from the Pentagon, so everyone thought they were real. I could get into anywhere.'

'What happened to all the stuff you downloaded? There wasn't room for it on your computer.'

'That was easy. I stored it at an Internet service in New York. It's called Mindvox. When I wanted to look at it, I just downloaded it from there.'

'And what about the power plant in Korea?'

'I wanted to have a go at a different sort of computer. I just tapped in the name of a Korean computer system. But I didn't hack into it.'

'OK,' said Agent Field. 'Just one more question. Who is Kuji?'

7

Date: Friday, 13 May 1994
Time: 09.00 hours
Location: New Scotland Yard, London, UK

Chief Inspector Lang and Sergeant Morris were meeting with Agent Field. They were discussing what Richard Pryce had told them the night before.

'Where is he now?' asked Agent Field.

'He's gone home,' said Sergeant Morris. 'We couldn't keep a 16-year-old locked up all night. Once we've decided what to charge him with, we'll pick him up again. We'll be watching him. Right now, he's banned from owning a computer.'

'The thing I find strange is how easy it was for him to break into the Pentagon computer,' said the Chief Inspector.

Agent Field frowned. 'To tell you the truth, it puzzles me too,' he said. 'But we've found out how he got the Carmen password.'

'Oh yes?'

'It seems that one US Air Force officer kept forgetting his code. So he changed it to Carmen. It's the name of his pet ferret.'

'That officer has cost us all a good deal of time and money,' said the Chief Inspector. 'Now, where are we getting with Kuji? I'm sure he's the brains behind all this. He was using Richard Pryce to find out what he wanted to know. He didn't want to hack into the system himself. He didn't want us to find him.'

Sergeant Morris answered. 'Pryce sent messages to Kuji through computer chat rooms. He's given us a phone number. He said he wasn't sure about it. We've tried it, but it turned out to be a girls' school.'

'So, how long is it going to take to find this Kuji?'

'I'm working on it. I'll be looking at every file on Pryce's computer. It'll take time, though.'

#

Date: Thursday, 20 June 1996
Time: 13.00 hours

Two years later, Richard Pryce was charged. He'd given the police all the information they'd asked for, but they still hadn't found Kuji.

'He used to help me when I got stuck,' Richard had said. 'In return, I passed onto him anything I found out.'

Sergeant Morris decided to have another look at Richard Pryce's computer files. After three weeks, he asked to see Chief Inspector Lang.

'I've had another look at those files,' he said. 'I don't know how I missed it the first time.'

He passed Lang a scrap of paper. Lang looked at it. He saw the name Kuji. There was a phone number next to it.

'Good work, Morris! What country? USA? China?'

Sergeant Morris faced him across the desk. 'No. He lives in Wales.'

Chief Inspector Lang made some quick phone calls. A small house in Cardiff was staked out. Who was Kuji? Who was he working for?

The next day, they found out. Kuji's real name was Matthew Bevan. He worked on computers for a local company. The 21-year-old wasn't a real spy either. Like Richard, he only wanted to find out if the US Government had a secret file on aliens!

Bevan was asked to go to the boss's office to check a computer. When he got there, he found the room was full of policemen. One of them stepped forward.

'Mr Bevan? Would you mind coming to the police station? We'd like to ask you a few questions.'

9

Date: Monday, 8 July 1996
Location: Bow Street Magistrates Court, London, UK

Richard wasn't feeling too good when he got to the court with his mother. Things looked bad. He didn't want to end up in a youth prison.

At the back of the court was a person he'd never seen before. Richard's solicitor pointed him out. 'That's Matthew Bevan.'

'You'd better go and shake hands,' said Mrs Pryce.

So, Datastream Cowboy and Kuji met face to face for the first time. They spoke very little. They couldn't think of much to say.

Thirteen charges were read out one by one. Richard was charged mainly with the illegal use of computers. There was one more charge of plotting with Matthew Bevan. Pryce pleaded guilty to the charges of computer misuse. His solicitor spoke up for him.

'The US Government was told in 1996 that Datastream Cowboy, or Richard Pryce, had done more harm than the Russian KGB. They said he was the "number one threat to the United States". I believe this claim is false. If a

16-year-old with very little know-how and a cheap computer can break the Pentagon network, something is wrong with that network! The US Government has given no proof that any real harm was done. I take this to mean that he did very little harm at all. He's a young man. He's not been in trouble before. So I hope the court will not be too hard on him.'

The solicitor knew he'd spoken well. If the US Government wanted to prove any harm had been done, they'd have to tell the court what secrets Richard had found out. They weren't going to do that.

In the end, Richard was fined £1,200. That was a hundred pounds for each charge of illegal use of computers. It was a lot of money for a 16-year-old to find. But he knew he'd been let off lightly. The charges of plotting with Bevan were dropped.

Richard Pryce decided there and then to have no more to do with computers. 'Hacking's a waste of time,' he said afterwards. 'From now on I'm sticking to music.'

Matthew Bevan stayed with computers. But not as a hacker. He made good use of all he'd learned. He got a job testing computer safety for private firms.

10

Matthew Bevan and Richard Pryce got off very lightly. Other computer hackers haven't been so lucky. A few years before, Kevin Mitnick from California had been hunted by the police all over America. He had used the name Condor for his hacking.

He'd caused even more problems than Richard and Matthew. He ended up with his face on a 'wanted' poster in every American police station. For most of his time as a hacker, he didn't even own a computer. He used computers in computer shops.

When the police caught Kevin he wasn't let off with a fine. He was sent to prison for 12 months.

Richard Pryce could hack computers because he could make free phone calls. He used special software for this. The software made the sound of a whistle down the phone. The sound had to be just right to work. Computer hackers call this 'phreaking' ('free-king').

An American called John Draper was the first to find this out. When he opened a packet of Cap'n Crunch breakfast cereal one morning, he found a toy whistle inside. He tried blowing it down the phone. It made the right sound to let him make a free phone call as long as he used the right software. After this, software that made the right sound was used instead of the whistle. Draper's hacking name was Cap'n Crunch!

When Richard Pryce started hacking, he found there were different kinds of hackers. Some were experts at writing software. Richard downloaded software from 'phreakers' so he could make free phone calls.

Next, he needed to break into a system. To do this he was helped by another group. They were called 'Crackers'. Then, he had to break secret codes. He learnt how to do this from hackers called 'cypherpunks' ('sifer-punks').

Most hackers break into computers for fun. But some are mixed up in crime. The Russian, Vladimir Levin, was not a teenager playing on a home computer. He was an expert in maths. He was also the leader of a computer-crime gang. He broke into the computer system of a bank. He tricked it into paying the gang ten million dollars. He thought he'd got away with it, but he left too many clues. The police arrested him in London in 1995.

People that harm other computers are a problem. The way they do this is by sending a computer virus across the Internet.

A virus is a small computer program. A computer program tells a computer to do something. This might be adding numbers together or checking spellings. A virus might make a computer do something else. It might make a silly message come up on the screen. It could do something much worse like tell a computer to wipe out all the information stored in it.

People who spread computer viruses have learnt a new trick. They tell the virus to look for all the e-mail addresses stored in a computer. The virus sends itself to all those addresses. In a few hours, the virus can travel the world. People open the e-mails because they think they come from someone they know.

During 1999 there were two big computer viruses, Melissa and LoveBug. The LoveBug virus sent a message saying 'I love you'. Everybody opened the message because they wanted to know who'd sent it. When they did, the virus ended up in their computer.

Both the Melissa and LoveBug viruses did a lot of harm. Most people are careful. They use anti-virus programs. The trouble is, the viruses (and the people who make them) are getting more clever!

It is hard to catch people who make viruses. Sometimes people take a program written by someone else and change it. It might be a different person who sends out the virus.

Richard and Matthew were hacking for fun. Richard told the

police it was just a game. He'd wanted to see how far he could go. Now criminals are learning the tricks that hackers like Richard and Matthew knew. People buy things on the Internet. Some crooks would like to help themselves to the money in other people's bank accounts.

It's not surprising that hackers like Matthew Bevan are now 'wanted', but not by the police. They are wanted by computer firms because they are experts in computer hacking.

Matthew and others like him now help to make the Internet safe. But for how long?

This book made use of newspaper articles of the period, including Jonathan Ungoed-Thomas in *The Sunday Times*, 30 March 1998. Other information can be found on Internet websites such as:

- The Hacker's Hall of Fame
  (www.discovery.com/area/technology/hackers/zero.html)

- So You Wanna be a Hacker?
  (www.ao.net/~cyberwar/hacker.html).